Exploring the Outdoors

Mountain Biking

Michael De Medeiros

MEDIA ENHANCED BOOKS
AV2
BY WEIGL™
ADDED VALUE • AUDIO VISUAL

www.av2books.com

AV² provides enriched content that supplements and complements this book
Weigl's AV² books strive to create inspired learning and engage young minds
in a total learning experience.

Your AV² Media Enhanced books come alive with...

Audio
Listen to sections of
the book read aloud.

Key Words
Study vocabulary, and
complete a matching
word activity.

Video
Watch informative
video clips.

Quizzes
Test your knowledge.

Embedded Weblinks
Gain additional information
for research.

Slide Show
View images and
captions, and prepare
a presentation.

Try This!
Complete activities and
hands-on experiments.

... and much, much more!

Go to **www.av2books.com**,
and enter this book's
unique code.

BOOK CODE

K495737

AV² by Weigl brings you media
enhanced books that support
active learning.

Published by AV² by Weigl
350 5th Avenue, 59th Floor
New York, NY 10118

Website: www.av2books.com   www.weigl.com

Library of Congress Cataloging-in-Publication Data
De Medeiros, Michael.
Mountain biking / Michael De Medeiros.
    p. cm. -- (Exploring the outdoors)
Includes index.
Summary: "Provides information about leisure activities that can be enjoyed in nature. Contains photos, charts, and healthy
eating and exercise tips that encourage readers to get outdoors and enjoy mountain biking"--Provided by publisher.
ISBN 978-1-62127-358-5 (hardcover : alk. paper) -- ISBN 978-1-62127-364-6 (softcover : alk. paper)
1. Mountain biking--Juvenile literature. I. Title.
GV1056.D393 2013
796.63--dc23
                         2012044678

Printed in the United States of America in North Mankato, Minnesota
1 2 3 4 5 6 7 8 9 0 17 16 15 14 13

012013
WEP301112

Project Coordinator: Alexis Roumanis
Art Director: Terry Paulhus

Every reasonable effort has been made to trace ownership and to obtain permission to reprint copyright material. The publisher
would be pleased to have any errors or omissions brought to their attention so that they may be corrected in subsequent printings.

Photo Credits
Weigl acknowledges Getty Images as the primary photo supplier for this title.

CONTENTS

All About Mountain Biking

Since the first bicycle was built, people have been riding bikes in the mountains. However, modern mountain biking first became known as a sport in the 1970s. Many people believe the sport first developed in California.

In the late 1960s, mountain bikers rode klunker bikes. Klunker bikes were old **cruiser** bikes with added homemade parts, fat tires, and better brakes. Cyclists would race down short, steep hills, dirt roads, and mountain trails. They timed themselves to see who could race downhill the fastest.

Mountain bikes have up to 30 gears allowing them to climb steep hills.

Some mountain bikers can perform tricks while riding.

Mountain biking has become more than a fun activity for people of all ages. It is a sport practiced around the world. There are national competitions in almost every country and several international competitions, such as the Olympic Games.

Mountain biking continues to become more popular. Each year, many people learn how to mountain bike. They consider it a fun way to keep fit and a challenging sport in which to compete.

CHANGES THROUGHOUT THE YEARS				
PAST	Riders moved bicycles by pushing the ground with their feet.	Bicycles had only one gear.	Women's bikes had a low top bar so that they could wear skirts while cycling.	People did not use safety gear while cycling.
PRESENT	Mountain bikes and other modern bikes have pedals.	Most mountain bikes have between 21 and 27 gears, though some have fewer and others have more.	Both men and women ride bikes with high top bars and wear shorts or pants.	Most people wear a helmet and reflectors while cycling.

Getting Started

Mountain biking can be dangerous. It is important to have the proper equipment to enjoy a safe ride. Having the right bike to ride is an important part of mountain biking.

A mountain bike is different from a road bike. A mountain bike must work well on bumpy, wet mountain trails. It has a strong frame that will not bend or break from rough use. The fatter tires on a mountain bike grip the ground better than thin road tires. Mountain bikes also have more gears, to adjust to the ever-changing terrain, or ground.

Mountain bikes are lower to the ground so that the rider is closer to the trail. He or she will be more stable and less likely to fall. A mountain bike's handlebars are raised higher than those of a road bike. This makes it easier to pull up on the handlebars and lift the front end of the bike over rocks, tree roots, or other objects on a trail.

Mountain bikers should wear tight clothing to prevent fabric from rubbing against the skin as they ride.

All the Right Equipment

1 A helmet will protect a rider's head if he or she falls off the bike.

2 Special mountain biking gloves are important. Gloves will protect hands from being scratched while riding or during a fall. Gloves also give the rider a better grip on the handlebars.

3 Sunglasses will keep the sunlight, dirt, bugs, and wind from getting in a rider's eyes.

4 A trail repair kit can help fix tires, brakes, and other parts that might become damaged during a ride. A mini air pump for easy tire **inflation** should be part of every trail repair kit.

5 Reflectors or reflective clothing will ensure that riders can be seen by other bikers or people. This will help the rider avoid accidents on the trail.

6 In warm weather, padded mountain bike shorts make the ride more comfortable. In cold and wet weather, riders should wear a waterproof jacket, winter tights, boots, and winter gloves.

Mountain Biking Basics

Before beginning a mountain biking trip, riders should know basic biking moves and techniques. Knowing these basics will help riders stay safe and enjoy their trip.

First, it is necessary to know how to **mount** a mountain bike. To mount a bike, make sure that the seat, or saddle, is set at the right height. After sitting on the saddle, the rider should be able to reach the lowest pedal with only a slight bend in the knee. If the leg does not reach the pedal, the saddle is too high. If the leg is bent, the saddle is too low.

After adjusting the saddle, riders should check the gears. Higher gears make it easier to pedal. They are used for riding uphill. Lower gears make it harder to pedal. They are used for flat or downhill terrain.

Before a mountain bike trip, it is important to ensure the tires are properly inflated.

When riders reach a muddy, sandy, or wet patch of land, it is important to shift the bike into a higher gear. It is more difficult to pedal over muddy, sandy, or wet ground. Using a higher gear allows the rider to keep moving instead of becoming stuck. Mountain bikers should also know how to lean their weight to the back end of the bike. This will help the front wheel slide across the ground.

Mountain bikers should not grip the handlebars too tightly. This will make the upper body tense and tire the rider faster. Riders should place their thumbs below the handlebars, keep their elbows bent, and ensure their shoulders are loose.

Mountain bikers should shift gears before beginning a downhill or uphill ride. It is safest to change gears while on flat ground. This also helps reduce wear on the gears.

Mountain Biking Levels

Mountain biking can be difficult or easy, depending on the rider's experience and the difficulty of the trail. Riders can help to ensure a safe and fun mountain biking experience by being prepared with the proper equipment and training.

Planning a **route** based on how far mountain bikers want to ride is important. Most people enjoy afternoon, day, or weekend trips. After deciding the distance of a ride, it is important to plan breaks. Most riders plan their stops around the more difficult parts of their route. If the path is known to have wet or muddy areas, riders often stop at those points. These stops allow riders to rest before tackling a challenging part of the trail.

Learning to ride through mud and water takes practice. For beginning riders, it is best to avoid these conditions if possible.

Some mountain bike tires are less likely to puncture on rough terrain. They are made from the same material used in bulletproof vests.

Most mountain bike racing paths have sections for beginners and others for more experienced riders. Most experienced riders prefer specialized paths because they are more challenging. Specialized paths test many mountain biking skills, such as steering, speed, handling, and uphill and downhill riding.

Average Biking Distances for Experienced Riders

Afternoon
10 to 15 miles (16 to 24 kilometers)

Full-day with rest stops
20 to 25 miles (32 to 40 km)

Full-day, off-road trip
50 miles (80 km)

Staying Safe

Mountain biking can be fun and exciting, but it is an **extreme sport**. Riders need to know how to avoid hazards on trails and how they can best protect themselves from injury.

When riders travel over rough terrain, they may be thrown from the bike. Broken bones, scrapes, and bruises are all risks of a challenging ride. All riders should carry a basic first aid kit that has bandages, moist towelettes, and scissors.

When braking, be sure to pull both the front and back brakes at the same time. Pulling only the front brake may cause the bike to tip forward, throwing the rider over the handlebars.

Riders should know their abilities and keep to paths that are not too difficult for their skill level. It is important to know where the path leads and how long it will take to ride from beginning to end. This will ensure that riders do not become lost and are not out at night when the trail is hard to see. Proper planning will help riders finish their routes.

Like any outdoor activity, mountain biking is affected by the weather. It is more difficult to bike in wet, muddy conditions. Riders should check local weather reports before riding. Try to plan trips on warm, sunny days.

Biking Tip #2

Plan your route carefully before taking a bike ride. Carrying a compass and a map can help show the way home if you become lost. Make sure to tell another person where you are going and when you plan to return.

Important Biking Supplies

Extra Clothing   Water   First Aid Kit

Explore the Outdoors

There are many other ways to explore the outdoors in the mountains. These activities include mountain climbing, snowboarding, bicycle motocross racing, and cycling.

Mountain Climbing

Mountain climbing, which is sometimes called mountaineering, is the act of climbing mountains, rocks, and ice. Climbing requires special equipment, such as ropes and harnesses, to keep climbers safe. People climb for sport, research, or recreation.

Snowboarding

Snowboarding is similar to skiing. However, snowboarders use one wide board instead of two long, thin skis. Snowboarders ride down snow-covered runs on ski hills. Like surfing and skateboarding, snowboarding became common in the United States in the 1980s. It was accepted into the Olympics in 1998 as a competitive sport.

Bicycle Motocross Racing

Bicycle motocross, or BMX, racing is a combination of mountain biking and cycling. It is an extreme sport. Racers wear helmets that cover their faces. They also wear padding that acts as a suit of protective armor. BMX racing often takes place on sand tracks that have large hills, ramps, and other obstacles.

Cycling

Cycling is the oldest sport that uses a bicycle. Cyclists take part in races on **closed courses** around the world. Cycling can be a team or single-person sport. Cyclists can reach speeds of more than 70 miles (113 kilometers) per hour. The Tour de France is the biggest international cycling competition. There are also cycling competitions in the Olympics.

Mountain Biking Around the World

1 Seven Summits Trail, Canada
One of the most adventurous mountain biking areas in the world, Seven Summits has more than 19 miles (30 km) of trails.

2 Moab, United States
Canyon country in Moab, Utah, has areas of desert and mountain terrain, sandstone arches, and large canyons.

3 Falun, Sweden
Although not as hilly as some areas, Falun includes long-distance trails and challenging terrain, such as rocks and exposed tree roots.

4 Swiss Alps, Switzerland
This area is known for its challenging trails and spectacular views. A tour of the Swiss Alps is considered by many riders to be an ideal mountain bike trip.

Arctic Ocean

1 Seven Summits Trail, Canada

North America

Atlantic Ocean

2 Moab, United States

Pacific Ocean

South America

N

SCALE

0 — 600 miles
0 — 1,000 Kilometers

Southern Ocean

M ountain biking can be done in almost every country in the world. Some riders like to plan routes in different cities, traveling many miles to view unique scenery and terrain. The following mountain biking areas are thought to be among the best in the world.

Join the Club

The International Mountain Bicycling Association (IMBA) is one of the best-known mountain biking associations in the world. The association was formed in 1988. Five riding clubs in California joined together to form the IMBA. The clubs were the Off Road Bicyclists Association, Bicycle Trails Council Marin, Bicycle Trails Council East Bay, Responsible Organized Mountain Pedalers, and Sacramento Rough Riders.

The IMBA works to create and preserve mountain biking trails all over the world. It encourages volunteer trail work and **low-impact** riding. The IMBA also works to keep trails open to riders. It has more than 32,000 members around the world.

Competitive international mountain biking began at the 1990 Mountain Bike World Championships. Since then, the sport has grown quickly and gained many fans. Mountain biking became an Olympic competition during the 1996 Atlanta Olympic Games. At the Olympics, riders compete in a cross-country mountain biking event. They must cross 25 to 30 miles (40 to 50 km) of rugged terrain, with hills, rocks, trees, and streams. The event takes athletes more than 2 hours to finish.

Riding clubs encourage mountain bikers to ride together in a group. This can be a way for beginners to learn from more experienced riders.

In the French Alps, riders participate in the Megavalanche Alpe d'Huez. It is a 20-mile (32-km) downhill race that starts in a glacier and ends in a wooded area.

Healthy Habits

A balanced diet is the first step towards a healthy and active lifestyle. Meals that include the four food groups give mountain bikers the minerals and energy they need to enjoy a full day of riding. The four food groups are dairy, grains, vegetables and fruits, and protein.

While riding, it is important to stay hydrated. This means riders must drink water often. Not all water is safe to drink. Some sources of water may carry **bacteria** that can cause illness. Mountain bikers should bring a supply of water. They should not drink from lakes or streams.

Mountain bikers need to maintain their physical fitness. They must have well-developed leg muscles to pedal the bike. Fit arms are needed to steer. A strong back helps to balance riders on bumpy trails.

Before taking mountain biking trips, there are a few basic warmup exercises that riders should perform. They are the knee bend, side stretch, spine reflex, and thigh stretch. These basic stretching exercises loosen muscles, which helps prevent injuries.

Eating protein, such as chicken, with a serving of fresh fruits or vegetables, will give bikers the necessary energy to mountain bike.

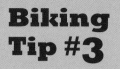

Biking Tip #3

When biking in the Sun for more than 30 minutes, it is important to use sunscreen.

It is important to walk or jog for a few minutes prior to stretching. This will warm up the muscles.

Stretches

Try practicing these stretches before biking to improve flexibility and prevent injury. Be sure to hold each stretch for 15 seconds.

Knee Bend
Stand with one hand holding onto a chair or other object for balance. Bend the right leg, and grasp the foot with the right hand. Breathe out, and pull the foot towards the buttocks until a stretch is felt. Repeat with the left leg.

Side Stretch
Point your left arm toward the ceiling. Place your right hand on your hip. Bend your body to the right. Repeat with your right arm in the air, and bend to the left.

Spine Reflex
Lean back without lying down to balance the weight of your legs.

Thigh Stretch
Stand with one leg in front of the other. Lean your upper body forward on the front leg. Repeat with the other leg in front.

Brain Teasers

Test your mountain biking knowledge by trying to answer these brain teasers.

Q How should mountain bikers grip the handlebar?

A: They should have their thumbs below the handlebars, elbows bent, and shoulders loose. Riders should not grip the bar too tightly.

Q When riding on a trail, what are some of the items riders should carry?

A: Riders should carry extra clothing, water, a first aid kit, and a trail repair kit.

Q Why do mountain bikers wear reflectors?

A: Mountain bikers wear reflectors to make sure they can be seen by other people. This helps them avoid accidents on the trail.

Q What five riding clubs created the International Mountain Bicycling Association?

A: The five clubs that joined together to form the IMBA were the Off Road Bicyclists Association, Bicycle Trails Council Marin, Bicycle Trails Council East Bay, Responsible Organized Mountain Pedalers, and Sacramento Rough Riders.

Q Where do most riders plan their stops on a route?

A: Most mountain bikers plan their stops around the difficult parts of their route.

Q What were early mountain bikes called?

A: Early mountain bikes were called klunkers.

Key Words

bacteria: organisms that spread disease

closed courses: courses for competition that only those competing can enter

cruiser: a balloon-tired bike with a heavy duty frame that was popular in the United States from the 1930s to 1970s

extreme sport: difficult or dangerous activity

inflation: the amount of air in a tire

low-impact: not damaging to the environment

mount: the act of getting into a seated position on a mountain bike

route: the path or trail a mountain biker rides

Index

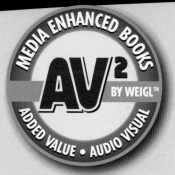

Log on to www.av2books.com

AV² by Weigl brings you media enhanced books that support active learning. Go to www.av2books.com, and enter the special code found on page 2 of this book. You will gain access to enriched and enhanced content that supplements and complements this book. Content includes video, audio, weblinks, quizzes, a slide show, and activities.

AV² Online Navigation

Book Pages
AV² pages directly correspond to pages in the book.

Audio
Listen to sections the book read alou

Video
Watch informative video clips.

Key Words
Study vocabulary, and complete a matching word activity.

Embedded Weblinks
Gain additional information for research.

Quizzes
Test your knowledge.

Slide Show
View images and captions, and prepare a presentation.

Try This!
Complete activities and hands-on experiments.

AV² was built to bridge the gap between print and digital. We encourage you to tell us what you like and what you want to see in the future.

Sign up to be an AV² Ambassador at www.av2books.com/ambassador.